REAL JUSTICE:

SENTENCED TO LIFE AT SEVENTEEN

• • •

THE STORY OF DAVID MILGAARD

CYNTHIA J. FARYON

LORIMER

JAMES LORIMER & COMPANY LTD., PUBLISHERS
TORONTO

James Lorimer & Company Ltd., Publishers acknowledges the support of the Ontario Arts Council. We acknowledge the financial support of the Government of Canada through the Canada Book Fund for our publishing activities. We acknowledge the support of the Canada Council for the Arts which last year invested $24.3 million in writing and publishing throughout Canada. We acknowledge the Government of Ontario through the Ontario Media Development Corporation's Ontario Book Initiative.

Library and Archives Canada Cataloguing in Publication

Faryon, Cynthia J., 1956-
    Real justice : sentenced to life at seventeen : the story of David Milgaard / Cynthia J. Faryon ; foreword by Win Wahrer.

(Real justice)
Includes bibliographical references and index.
Issued also in electronic format.
ISBN 978-1-55277-433-5 (pbk.). --978-1-4594-0169-3 (bound)

    1. Milgaard, David, 1952- --Juvenile literature. 2. Murder--Saskatchewan--Saskatoon--Juvenile literature. 3. Judicial error--Canada--Juvenile literature. I. Title. II. Title: Sentenced to life at seventeen.

HV6535.C33S36 2012   j364.15'23092   C2009-904311-4

James Lorimer & Company Ltd.,
Publishers
317 Adelaide Street West, Suite 1002
Toronto, ON, Canada
M5V 1P9
www.lorimer.ca

Distributed in the United States by:
Orca Book Publishers
P.O. Box 468
Custer, WA, USA
98240-0468

Printed and bound in Canada.
Manufactured by Friesens Corporation in Altona, Manitoba, Canada in August 2012.
Job #77085

IN MEMORY OF MY HUSBAND, ROGER FONTAINE,
WHO LOST HIS BATTLE WITH CANCER ON
DECEMBER 15, 2010.
HIS SUPPORT, OPINIONS, AND LOVE WILL BE MISSED.

CONTENTS

NOTE

Throughout this book, the author has endeavoured to use quoted dialogue wherever possible. The sources include: newspaper articles, trial transcripts, Inquiry reports and witness statements, police reports, and public documents, as well as other publications noted in the endnotes. When quoted dialogue is not available, a limited number of conversations have been reconstructed from the facts of the case, the evidence and reports, and the likelihood of the dialogue in order to help explain or highlight the facts of the story.

The dialogue in chapter one was created from the Inquiry and trial transcripts.

The murder re-enactment is an unconfirmed scenario based on the evidence and *testimony* given at the Inquiry. Larry Fisher has never admitted to killing Gail Miller.

The conversation between Ron and Nichol, which took place before the polygraph, and the interviews that followed were reconstructed from testimony taken from the Inquiry and from an investigation completed on June 18, 1992.

The letter dated May 1, 1981, was written by David Milgaard to Nichol (Niki) John and has been taken from the public documents used in the Commission of Inquiry Into the Wrongful Conviction of David Milgaard. In this letter David states he is twenty-five; however, as of the date on the letter, his actual age would have been twenty-eight.

The undated letter was written by David Milgaard to Albert Cadrain and has been taken from the public documents used in the Inquiry Into the Wrongful Conviction of David Milgaard.

FOREWORD

This book tells the true and tragic story of a young man who, through no fault of his own, was *convicted* at the age of seventeen of a heinous and brutal crime that he did not commit. It covers the long, arduous, and painful journey to his freedom and exoneration, which came at a very high personal cost to him and to those who loved and supported him. This is the true story of how the indomitable spirit of a young boy, and the heart and determination of a mother, can triumph over the mountain of roadblocks placed between them and the truth.

The Association in Defence of the Wrongly Convicted (AIDWYC) was formed in 1993 to review and access the merits of claims of innocence in homicide cases. David Milgaard was exonerated in 1997 as a result of *DNA* testing arranged through the AIDWYC. The AIDWYC received standing at the Inquiry into his wrongful conviction in 2005 and Joyce Milgaard was represented by two AIDWYC lawyers, Joanne McLean and James Lockyer, at the Inquiry.

Both Joyce and David Milgaard have taught me and countless others about faith, struggle, and determination. They've also taught us that if you persevere long enough, work hard enough, and count the sacrifices as blessings, if you don't give up and you are armed with the truth and the support of good people, anything is possible, even if the pursuit of justice does come at a high personal cost.

— Win Wahrer
Director of Client Services, AIDWYC

PROLOGUE

STALKER IN SASKATOON

OCTOBER 21, 1968: SASKATOON, SK

Larry Fisher watched the twenty-two-year-old woman come out of the store with a glass bottle of pop. He'd seen her before, watched her, followed her, but never talked to her. It was about 8 p.m. and already dark. Larry was still wearing his hard hat from work.

The girl didn't seem to notice Larry lurking outside the store, or when he fell in behind her. As they passed the entrance to a back lane, Larry grabbed her and shoved his dirty hand over her mouth. The woman struggled and tried to scream. The bottle of pop slipped out of her hand and shattered loudly on the sidewalk. There was a flash of silver as Larry pulled out his knife and pressed it against her chest.

"Don't you dare say anything," he hoarsely whispered into her ear. "Or I'll have you with this knife."

The girl tried to struggle but Larry was too strong for her. He pushed her into the alley. She twisted and he moved his hand from her mouth to her throat. Her glasses fell off. He stepped on them and ground them under his feet.

"Please, no," she pleaded. "My glasses — can I please get my glasses?"

"Never mind the glasses, keep going," he said and shoved her between two garages in the darkest part of the alley. He didn't have to worry about being interrupted here. He loosened his grip and she tried to turn her head to look at him, but he knew it was too dark to see him clearly.

"I've seen you around here — lots," he said.

"Where?" she whispered.

"Oh, around," Larry laughed and pushed her face down on the ground. He yanked her blouse over her head and forced part of it into her mouth so her screams would be muffled while he assaulted her.

• • •

A month later, on November 13, Larry Fisher was back at it. Again he wore his work clothes and hard hat. He worked as a labourer on a construction site at the University of Saskatchewan. It had been a very tough day and he was looking for recreation. Walking towards him on the sidewalk was a seventeen-year-old girl he saw on the bus he rode home every day. He wasn't worried about her recognizing him. He knew that girls like her never looked at guys like him. They noticed the guys attending the university — not the grunts like him without money or an education.

Larry watched her walk towards him. His breathing quickened. As she passed by, he swung around and grabbed her from behind. He put one hand over her mouth and pressed a knife to her throat — hard enough to make a dent, but not enough to pierce her skin.

"If you want to live then do as I say," he said.

Larry dragged her into a dark yard. He was rough and smelled of oil. "Don't scream, lie still, don't move."

The girl, terrified Larry would kill her if she disobeyed, did as she was told.

• • •

Two weeks later, Larry Fisher attacked another young woman on her way home from the University of Saskatchewan library.

The police were baffled. They believed the same man committed all the attacks, but none of the victims or witnesses were able to give them a good description of him, other than that he wore work clothes and a hard hat, and he used a knife.

The police handed out flyers. The newspapers and television and radio stations warned the public of a rapist in the Pleasant Hill and university areas of Saskatoon. Someone out there knew this man, and the police hoped they could put him behind bars before he escalated and seriously hurt someone.

They would be too late.

1

CHAPTER ONE

A BAD IDEA

JANUARY 1969: REGINA, SK

"My buddy Shorty loves road trips and he's always got a load of cash. I can get him to pay for the trip and the dope," David Milgaard said to his friends Ron Wilson and Nichol John.

"Saskatoon?" said Ron. "We're in Regina. That's a long way to go with almost no cash only to find out he's not into it."

"He'll be cool, you'll see," David assured him.

With his thick black hair, expressive eyes, and warm smile, David Milgaard could be almost irresistible when he turned on the charm. The sixteen-year-old was living the life many teenagers dreamed of; he had his own place and a job where he earned his own money, which he spent as fast as he made. There were no curfews or boundaries in David's life. Nothing was forbidden — not drugs or girls or petty theft. (And at five foot ten with an athletic build, David was the kind of guy some girls noticed.) The only people he had to watch out for were the police.

"Come on, Ron. It'll be a blast."

David had met Ron Wilson a year before at a race track in Regina. When the car Ron was riding in had driven by, Ron's naked rear-end had been hanging out the window. The "mooning" caught David's attention and he made the effort to get to know him.

The two had clicked. They had similar experiences. When David was younger, his parents couldn't handle him, so he'd landed in foster care and then juvenile detention for petty theft and for joyriding in a stolen car. In a separate incident, Ron had received a jail sentence for breaking and entering and was out on probation. They were on common ground. Neither of them wanted to ever be locked away again, but they were still teenagers looking for a good time.

"Hey! Road trip?" said Nichol John. "It'll be awesome. I'm coming, right? You guys can't leave me here in this dump."

For sixteen-year-old Nichol John, drugs were a regular part of her day. Acid, hash, pot — she wasn't fussy. Nichol had been unhappy at home and kept running away. She was living at a friend's house and worked as a waitress after blowing off school. She was on her own and really, no one cared where she got her money and she didn't answer to anyone. There was always some guy willing to buy lunch or drugs, or both, for favours. Her friends were her family now.

"Yeah," said David. "You have to come. We guys need entertaining."

David was handsome and Nichol was cute, and the attraction had been immediate and mutual. Even though she had been Ron's girlfriend, soon Nichol was bouncing from one boy to the next and then back again. No one cared. It was fun and games.

That January, the three teens had been partying for a couple of weeks, until most of the money and drugs had run out. David had just come up with a crazy plan to get both money and drugs. He thought if they could get to his friend Shorty's house in Saskatoon, then Shorty (aka Albert Cadrain) would give them money to drive out to Vancouver to hook up with a drug dealer David knew.

Ron was the only one who owned a vehicle and there wouldn't be a road trip if Ron didn't go. Finally, David convinced him. But Ron's old Pontiac wasn't in great shape. None of them had enough money to fix it and still go on the trip. They found a parked car in a dark driveway and stole its battery and siphoned the gas tank. Hooking up the stolen battery in the cold, dark January night was messy and frustrating, and battery acid was spilled on David's pants. David also somehow ripped his pants in the crotch, which made the three of them laugh hysterically.

Nichol was the only clean one, since she was holding the flashlight.

"Okay, so we got a tank of gas, but I don't know where we'll get our next one," said David.

"Look for a lady with a purse," answered Ron.

By the time they climbed into the car and rolled out of Regina, headed for Saskatoon, the weather had turned nasty. It was nearly 1 a.m., but none of them cared. They were young, they could handle anything.

2

CHAPTER TWO

ROAD TRIP

JANUARY 31, 1969: HIGHWAY 11, BETWEEN
REGINA AND SASKATOON, SK

It's 235 kilometres from Regina to Saskatoon. David,
Ron, and Nichol barely had enough money to make it
there, and no money to make it back. They were without
a map. They were riding in a beat-up, two-tone Pontiac
relic. It had bald summer tires and a heater that only
worked now and then. But they weren't worried. They
were having a laugh, smoking dope, and pushing the
car out of the ditch when it slid off the icy road. They
didn't have a shovel, so the three of them dug the tires
out of the snow with their bare hands. It was funny the
first time, less funny the second. The third time? Not so
much. Along the way they made a pit stop by some train
tracks near Aylesbury so Nichol could relieve herself in
a snow bank. While the others waited, David broke into

a nearby grain elevator and brought back a flashlight, which was all he could find to steal. At minus 42 degrees, it was lung-burning cold. It was windy and snow blew everywhere, swirling across the road and making it hard to see. By the time they reached the town of Davidson, halfway between Regina and Saskatoon, they were cold and hungry. They stopped for coffee and hoped Shorty would feed them when they landed at his door.

"Are we gonna score some stuff in Saskatoon? Ya know, before we get to Vancouver?" Nichol asked. She really wanted to get high, acid high; all they had were a few joints of pot.

"Yeah, Niki," said David. "Shorty'll hook us up."

But David only sort of knew where Shorty lived, since he'd been to the house only once. He didn't have the address or the phone number but thought the neighbourhood was called "hill" something. The three teens drove all night, and at 6:30 a.m. on a foggy Friday morning, they arrived in Saskatoon and began the search for Shorty's house.

• • •

Larry Fisher knew where Shorty Cadrain lived. Larry lived in the basement apartment of the Cadrain house with his wife and young child. That morning Larry was parked in a borrowed two-tone Chevy just seven blocks away from the house, which was in the Pleasant Hill neighbourhood of the city.

The girl Larry was watching this time was walking towards the bus stop at Avenue O and 20th Street. He'd seen her on the bus to the university many times and knew her route. It was the same bus he took to get to work each day.

He got out of the car and walked into a yard and looked up the lane. There she was, coming towards him. He gripped his knife tightly and took a step forward.

The girl moved closer to the fence, but Larry wouldn't be put off. He walked straight up to her and grunted at her. For a moment the girl looked confused and seemed to hesitate. She looked around to see if anyone could see what was happening, but they were alone. She tried to go around him, but Larry moved to block her path. Suddenly, he grabbed her and started pushing her towards the fence, grabbing at her clothes. She was carrying her books in front of her with her lunch bag on top so she couldn't push him away. Larry got hold of her pants, but she was struggling too hard. This made him angry.

The girl screamed and threw her books into the air. Now startled, Larry walked away a few steps and paused, as though he might come at her again. The girl began to cry and call out for help. Larry turned quickly and ducked into an alley.

The girl hurried away. She didn't call the police right away to report the incident. She didn't call until she heard the disturbing news later in the day that a woman was found murdered only a few blocks away.

3

CHAPTER THREE

A CHANCE MEETING

JANUARY 31, 1969: 7 - 7:30 A.M.
SASKATOON, SK

The heater in Ron Wilson's car had stopped working again and frost was forming on the inside of the windows. David saw a garage, so they stopped to see if they could get the heater fixed. The garage wasn't able to help them, but the teens got pea soup out of a machine for 50 cents and waited a few minutes to warm up before getting back on the road. David thought they were in the right area of Shorty's house, but he wasn't sure exactly where it was. Ron was driving, and he was getting frustrated at David's confusion. They seemed to be going in circles.

David, Ron, and Nichol drove slowly down 20th Street looking for Shorty's house. David stared intently out the car window. He had no clue where they were or in which direction they should look. All the streets seemed to look alike in the snow and the car kept sliding sideways. Up ahead they saw a young woman hurrying along the sidewalk.

"Slow down, Ron," said David. "Pull over and I'll ask for directions."

"Hey, David," said Ron as they pulled up beside the woman. "Try to grab her purse after you ask her, cash is getting low."

"Excuse me, lady?" called David. "I'm looking for someone called Cadrain in the 'hill' area, you know, either Pleasant or Peace. Do you know the Cadrains?"

• • •

Gail Miller looked over at the three teens in the car. She was in a hurry and didn't have time for this. The night before she'd been at a birthday party, where she'd had too much to drink. She was tired from staying up until 3 a.m. the night before and feared she wouldn't get to the Avenue O stop in time to catch her bus. She shook her head: no, she didn't know the Cadrains.

Gail tightened her black coat against the weather and hurried to catch her regular bus that arrived between 7:10 and 7:15 a.m. It was horribly cold to travel by bus, especially while wearing her nurse's uniform: a dress and nylon stockings. A nursing assistant at City Hospital in Saskatoon, Gail's childhood dream had been to work as a nurse and care for children. The work was great, but the winter weather wasn't.

Gail was a hometown Saskatchewan girl from the small town of Delisle. As the second oldest in a family of nine children, her dream hadn't seemed possible until her grandmother helped her pay for her education.

She felt lucky to be living her dream and working in Saskatoon.

4

CHAPTER FOUR

MURDER

7:10 - 8 A.M.

Larry Fisher watched Gail walk away from the three teens in the Pontiac and disappear around a corner. He drove slowly, following her into an alley with the car headlights lighting up the dark. Gail turned and shaded her eyes against the glare. Larry got out of the car and grabbed her, putting his knife to her throat. She fought as he dragged her into the car.

• • •

"We need a map," said Nichol. "See anywhere we can get a map?"

Ron pulled into the parking lot of the Trav-a-Leer motel and David ran into the lobby to buy a map and ask for directions. David was shoeless and coatless, which the desk clerk thought odd. He jumped back into the car shaking with the cold and blowing heat into his hands, but now he knew where they were going. It was the Pleasant Hill neighbourhood.

"Turn here, Ron, down the alley . . . Stop, man!"

"Trying to stop . . . it's too slippery. Ya gotta tell me sooner."

"Man, you got to turn around; you passed it. Right here, Ron. Turn around here and go back to that alley."

Ron's car slid to the middle of the intersection and he yanked on the wheel to make a U-turn. The car zig-zagged in a half circle then ended up stuck in the snow. At least they were pointed in the right direction. David put on his coat and shoes and he and Ron tried to push the car out while Nichol sat behind the wheel. It wouldn't budge. David and Ron left Nichol in the car and went to look for help. They returned in a few minutes with two guys, who helped push them out.

Once again they tried to turn down the alley that would take them to Shorty's house. But they didn't get far. A convertible was stuck in the snow and blocked the route. It looked as though the driver had backed straight out and slid into the snowbank.

"Just back up, man, and turn around," David told Ron.

"Can't, reverse don't work," Ron replied. "My gears are stripped."

David and Ron got out of their car and tried to help the owner of the other vehicle — Walter Danchuk — push his car out, but after an hour and a half it still wasn't freed.

"Look, boys," Walter said. "You can't wait out here in this weather; the tow truck could take hours. Come inside my house to wait."

"Thank you, sir," said David. "That's really nice of you — as long as it isn't any trouble."

• • •

As he put the coat back on Gail's body, Larry Fisher thought about how he hadn't meant to kill her. He'd seen her talking to some kids in a car and she seemed an easy target.

Now he was panicking. He couldn't go to work, and he didn't want to go home and face his wife, Linda. She was already going to be mad at him for not coming home from work the night before. He needed to get rid of all this blood and return the car he had borrowed. Everything was a mess.

It was still dark outside. He ran around the front of the idling car to the passenger side and dragged Gail's body out. He dumped her down onto the snow. He had to disappear from here, and quickly. As he drove away, he realized some of her stuff was still in the car. He had to get rid of it. He began to throw anything that belonged to Gail out the window with the hope that it would remain buried in the snow until spring.

Larry pulled up in front of the Cadrain house. He still had Gail's wallet and a toque. He tossed them into the yard close to the neighbours but didn't realize he'd thrown his own wallet as well. He looked around to see if anyone had noticed him before getting out of the car.

Quietly, Larry crept into the basement. He didn't dare go through to the suite where he lived. Instead, he went to the laundry room so he could clean up before facing his wife. He undressed and left the pile of bloody clothes on the floor by the washing machine. Should he simply wash the clothes or get rid of them? And if he got rid of them, how could he do that so they wouldn't lead back to him?

He slipped into the shower in the bathroom next to the laundry room. He scrubbed hard at his body, removing all the blood and anything else that would tell where he'd been — and what he'd done.

CHAPTER FIVE

THE HOUSE IN PLEASANT HILL

8 - 9:30 A.M.

After breakfast, Shorty Cadrain's little sister, Rita, went downstairs to her bedroom in the basement to get dressed for school. She didn't like sleeping in the basement next to the suite. Larry Fisher was creepy. Linda and the baby were cool; it was just Larry.

Rita went into the laundry room to find a sweater and saw the pile of bloody clothes on the floor. It scared her. She ran out of the room and up the stairs.

Larry saw Rita as he came out of the bathroom. He would need to get out of the house, quickly. He didn't have time to get clean boots, so he slipped on the bloody ones. He threw his bloodied clothes in a plastic bag and ran out the door with them.

Running up the stairs as fast as she could, Rita burst into the kitchen and told her mom what she'd found.

Her mom laughed, but agreed to go to the laundry room and look.

The clothes were gone.

"I don't understand," said Rita, dumbfounded. "They were right here, Mom, they were."

"Rita, we've gone over this before. There's nothing wrong with the Fishers. You have to sleep in the basement bedroom no matter how much you don't like it. I don't want to hear your stories this morning. Now get ready for school."

• • •

David, Ron, and Nichol were really bored. They visited with the Danchuk family for almost an hour and a half. It was nice they let them stay warm in the house while they waited for the tow truck. But there was only so much they could talk about with strangers.

The tow truck finally arrived and pulled out the convertible that was blocking the alley. Ron, Nichol, and David got into their car to leave, but now it wouldn't start. They got a boost from the tow-truck driver.

"Okay, you're good to go," the tow-truck driver said to them. "The bill is three dollars."

"Ya got change for a ten?" asked Ron.

"Nope, I don't," said the driver.

"Okay, then how about we follow you to the gas

station and pay the bill there?" said David.

"Yeah, sure, that'll work."

But the tow truck drove off in one direction and Ron drove off in the other.

"I can't believe he fell for that," laughed Ron. They had no intention of paying the bill.

Following the map from the motel, David finally led them to the Cadrain house. While the others waited in the car, David approached the house to make sure it was okay for them all to come in.

6

CHAPTER SIX

DAVID IS MISSING

8:30 - 9:30 A.M.

After leaving the Cadrains', Larry returned the borrowed car to his wife's relative's place and left the key under the mat. He grabbed the bag containing his bloodied clothes and balled up a bloody blanket on the front seat of the car and tucked it under his arm. Then he walked the few blocks to Linda's uncle's house. There, in the backyard, he dumped the clothes and the blanket into a burning barrel and lit them on fire. Remembering his boots, Larry slipped them off and into the fire, too. He did the same with his coat.

Larry stayed next to the barrel long enough to make sure everything was burning before knocking on the back door of the house. His wife's uncle answered.

"Hey," Larry said. "Where were you? I knocked a couple of times and there was no answer." The uncle looked at him oddly. It was minus 42 degrees outside and Larry was standing there in the snow without shoes or a jacket.

"What happened, Larry?" The uncle could see the fire in the barrel.

"I was at a party and someone stole my coat and shoes. It must have been a joke, but I don't think it's very funny. You didn't answer when I knocked so I lit the fire in the barrel to keep warm." He was a good liar.

Larry stayed for a few minutes and then borrowed a coat and a pair of shoes so he could walk home.

• • •

Shorty opened the door and told David, Ron, and Nichol to come inside and his mother would make them breakfast.

"It [the house] was really messy. There was pots on the stove that were, umm, really disgusting." David said later. "It was old, like 1940s or 1950s."

Shorty was pumped; he really liked their idea of a road trip to Vancouver.

While Shorty packed a bag, David stole the car keys from Ron and decided to move the car into the drive-way and bring in a suitcase so he could change his pants, which were torn and stained red from battery acid.

But once he got behind the wheel, David wanted to

have some fun. He drove around the block a few times, spinning the car in circles on the icy roads and laughing. He was gone about fifteen minutes when suddenly the car stopped working altogether. Nothing worked; the motor wouldn't even turn over. There was transmission fluid all over the snow under the car. David knew he was in big trouble and walked a couple of blocks back to Shorty's.

Ron was furious. They called the nearby garage and got it towed there so it could be fixed. They were out of money, so Shorty agreed to pay for it.

Later that day, the teens were finally ready to continue on their trip. They left Saskatoon headed for adventure on their brief trip west. The stopover in Saskatoon had seemed so innocent to them then. In their minds it was just a road trip with a few laughs. No one got hurt, right? It wasn't like they killed anyone.

"We were just kids, on a lark, hippies," David said later. "What can I tell ya?"

7

CHAPTER SEVEN

PUTTING THE PIECES TOGETHER

Gail Miller's half-frozen body was found in the alley, the snow around her stained with blood, on the same day of her murder. Her nurse's uniform had been stripped off her upper body and she was only wearing one boot. She had been stabbed fourteen times through her coat, but the upper part of her uniform was free of knife cuts. Her throat had been slashed fifteen times.

This was the scene that a couple of young children happened upon around 8:30 a.m. on January 31, 1969, on their way to school. The kids ran for help and within ten minutes, Sergeant Reid and Detective Parker of the Saskatoon police arrived on the scene.

Even police detectives were shocked by the murder of Gail Miller. Sure, murder happened in Saskatoon, but in a quiet Prairie city such as this, there were only one or two homicides a year — and nothing so violent.

The crime scene was cordoned off and searched, a task that was made difficult by the snow. A broken knife blade covered in the victim's blood was found under the body and tagged as the murder weapon. Gail's sweater and her boot were found nearby on the grounds of a funeral home. Her purse was missing and would be found a few days later in a garbage can. In time, as the investigation at the crime scene continued, two frozen lumps of semen would also be discovered and sent to the lab.

Was the murder connected to the recent attacks on women in the neighbourhood? Police thought it most likely was. They canvassed the area. They questioned the residents of the boarding house where Gail lived. The night before her murder, they discovered, a two-toned car had been sitting outside the boarding house with its motor running. When Gail's date that evening had brought her home, the occupant of the car turned on its headlights, blinding her date so he couldn't see who was in the car.

Two days after the murder, police questioning people on the street caught up with Larry Fisher at his bus stop. Larry was on his way to work and wearing his yellow hard hat.

"Excuse me, sir?" Detective Parker said to Larry Fisher. "I don't know if you've heard, but there was a murder in the area a few days ago, and we're looking for anyone who may have seen anything out of the ordinary on the morning of January 31, at about 6:30 a.m."

"I don't remember seeing anything strange," said Larry. "Why at that time of the morning, Detective?"

"Well, that was approximately the time that Gail Miller left for work in the morning. She usually caught the bus here."

"And she never did show up, so that was on the thirty-first?" asked Larry.

"Right and your name is?"

"Larry Fisher. I live at 334 Avenue O South. I caught the bus here at that time on the thirty-first. If you want, you can check with my boss. I work at the Education Building; I do masonry construction. I'm sorry I can't give you any information. I really can't recall seeing anything that morning."

"One more question, Mr. Fisher. Do you always wear your hard hat to work?"

"Yeah. I usually catch the bus right away. It saves me having to carry it with everything else. I wear it all the time when I go outside; I never wear a toque anyhow."

"Do you remember ever seeing some of the same people at the bus stop when you went to work in the morning?" asked the detective.

"I couldn't even tell you that."

"So you don't remember seeing a nurse on the same bus?"

"No, sir."

"How about another construction worker wearing a hard hat?"

"No, sir."

"Do you own a car, Mr. Fisher?"

"No, sir."

With that, the officer scratched Larry off the list and moved on to question others nearby. The officer did not follow up with Larry's boss to see if he'd been at work on January 31. Nor did he go to Larry's home address. No one checked with Linda Fisher about her husband's whereabouts on the morning of the murder. They did not discover that he lived in the basement of Shorty Cadrain's house. They did not hear Rita's story about the bloody clothes in the laundry room.

If the town of Saskatoon, specifically the Pleasant Hill neighbourhood, had been concerned about the recent attacks on women, they were horrified by the news on the radio of the murder. They were even more horrified when the police were quoted in Saskatoon's *The StarPhoenix* on February 1 of the possibility that the murder was linked to those attacks.

The police gathered information and followed leads on more than 200 persons of interest. They made a list of possible murderers. They learned of Les Spence, Gail's ex-boyfriend. He was known to have a bad temper, and the couple had split after he had hit her. Les had wanted Gail back and would sometimes follow her. On February 4, 1969, police found Les Spence and interviewed him. He had an alibi and witnesses for the time of the murder. They were also able to verify that his car was in the shop for repairs on January 31. The ex-boyfriend was crossed off the list of suspects.

People at the party Gail had been to the night before her murder were tracked down and interviewed. But everywhere the police came up short.

They were left with two possibilities: either the driver of the car parked outside the boarding house the night of the party had murdered her or the murder was connected to the recent rapes. Neither led them to Larry Fisher, the real killer.

8

CHAPTER EIGHT

THE WRONG LEAD

On February 6, 1969, a chain of events began that ulti-
mately set the police on the wrong path in their investigation — a path that took them to David Milgaard.

Shorty Cadrain was arrested by the Regina City
Police for vagrancy (being homeless). Shorty told the
Regina police he was from Saskatoon. By now people in
Regina were well aware of the murder of Gail Miller in
Saskatoon. The police interviewed Shorty in connection
with the murder and asked him about his whereabouts
that day. Shorty told them that David Milgaard and his
friends had arrived the same morning of the murder and
that they left town later that day. He told them they were
driving a two-tone Pontiac. He also told them about
David's job travelling all over Saskatchewan selling magazine subscriptions door-to-door.

Shorty denied that any of them were involved in

the murder. But Regina police contacted the Saskatoon police anyway, and told them what they had found out. Detectives there decided they wanted to talk to David Milgaard, Ron Wilson, and Nichol John.

Meanwhile, back in Saskatoon, a couple of detectives visited the Cadrain house and spoke to Shorty's mother. She told them that her son didn't have anything to do with the murder, that he and his friends had gone west, and as far as she knew, Shorty had gone to Regina afterwards. She had no idea where David, Ron, and Nichol were. The police didn't ask her if anyone other than her family lived in the house and she didn't tell the police about the basement suite where the Fishers lived. Rita was at school. Her mother didn't tell the police about the bloody clothing her daughter said she found. She still wasn't sure if Rita had made it up, or if she really had seen it. Besides, if Rita had seen it, and she told the police about it, then they might think her son was the murderer. She kept quiet.

Shorty spent a week in a Regina jail before he was released. When he returned home, his mother was really upset. She told him the police had come and asked questions about his friends. They asked questions about the murder of Gail Miller on the morning they left town. She wanted to know if Shorty was involved. She also told him that the police were offering a $2,000 reward for information leading to an arrest and *conviction* of the person or persons responsible for the murder of Gail Miller.

Shorty tried to digest this information. He was having trouble sleeping and remembering things, and sometimes his mind was jumbled. He even heard voices. He didn't like the interrogation the police had given him, or spending time in jail. Everything bad that had happened to him lately had to do with David and his buddies. On the road trip, they had used up his cash and then left him to make his own way home.

His mind was spinning. He couldn't think. Had he seen blood on David's pants when he arrived at his doorstep? There had been something, but David had said it was battery acid. Then David had been gone a long time with Ron's car. Could David have done it?

By March 2, 1969, Shorty Cadrain had made up his mind. He called the police.

"Umm, hello?" He spoke nervously to the police officer on the telephone. He needed to get them off his back and he could use the reward money. He didn't seem to consider, or understand, the consequences of his phone call. It would be the worst decision of his life.

"Umm, my name is Shorty, um, Albert Cadrain. I

have information, man . . . I know who murdered Gail Miller. It was David Milgaard. I saw blood on his pants. But you can't let him know it was me who ratted. He's crazy. He's involved with the mafia. He'll kill me; ya gotta protect me."

Lorne and Joyce Milgaard on their wedding day.

David, age three, with his mother, Joyce.

Joyce Milgaard visits David at the Kingston Penitentiary.

David Milgaard was sixteen when he was arrested for murder.

Twenty-year-old Gail Miller was found murdered in January 1969.

David Milgaard at the time of his psychiatric examination.

Saskatchewan Penitentiary in Prince Albert, Saskatchewan.

David Milgaard walks with his mother and sister, Maureen, in 1991, the day after learning the Supreme Court would re-examine his 1970 murder conviction.

9

CHAPTER NINE

TRAIL OF EVIDENCE

David was in Winnipeg, Manitoba, with his sales manager. His job was selling magazine subscriptions. One
morning his manager knocked on the door of the motel
room where he was staying.

"David," he said. "The police are here. They want to
question you about a murder."

At first David thought his manager was kidding. But
the man looked serious.

David swallowed nervously. A murder! What could
he possibly know about a murder?

"Okay."

David went to the lobby where the police were waiting to take him to the police station. According to the
Criminal Code of Canada in 1969, the police had the
right to question anyone of interest in a criminal investigation, even a teenager without a parent or guardian

present. They were supposed to make every effort to locate a parent or guardian, though. Since David was working and living on his own, the police notified his parents only as a courtesy. David could have requested that his parents be present during the questioning. He didn't.

At the police station, David was nervous, but he knew he could handle this. After all, he hadn't done anything wrong.

"Mr. Milgaard, this is very serious. We need some samples from you: semen, blood, hair; is this okay?"

"Yeah, yeah, sure."

"So, Mr. Milgaard, may I call you David?"

"Sure."

"David, were you in Saskatoon this year?"

"Maybe," said David.

"When would you have been in Saskatoon?"

"I'm not sure."

"Okay, when you arrived in Saskatoon, was it daylight?"

"I think so," said David.

"Why can't you remember?"

"Time doesn't mean anything or days, maybe years." David smiled to himself. He was playing with them. They were grown-ups and thought they were in control, but they weren't. David was only sixteen and felt he was in control.

"After you got to Shorty's house, did you leave Shorty's by yourself and drive away?"

"Yeah, I turned the car around."

"Why?" asked the officer.

"It was across the street . . . I was putting it on the right side for the suitcases." David continued the game.

"Did you drive around the block?"

"Yeah, around up the lane, maybe twice."

"If you were tired and got stuck in the lane already, why did you go in the lane again?"

"I like to drive I guess," said David.

The police were getting frustrated.

"Someone told us you had blood on your clothes. Did you have blood on your clothes?"

"I don't know. I don't think so. I suppose you think I had something to do with the girl?"

The officers looked at David with interest. David suddenly felt sick to his stomach. Maybe he shouldn't have let them know he knew about the murder.

"What girl?" the officer asked carefully.

The room was suddenly quiet. The wall clock ticked and one of the officers, who had been tapping his pen against the desk, stopped. They were all staring at David.

He paused while he tried to swallow the lump in his throat.

"Gail Miller," he said. It was serious now. The game wasn't fun anymore. David didn't feel like playing with the cops any longer. At first the questions were a way to be a smart-ass. This was different.

"Where did you hear that name?" the officer asked.

"The RCMP guy, the guy who picked me up from the motel, he told me about her being killed."

When David left the police station a few hours later he hoped that would be the last he'd hear of the Gail Miller murder. He was wrong.

The following day, the police caught up with Ron Wilson. He was interviewed in Regina. Ron told the detective exactly what had happened on their trip to Saskatoon. He also stated that he didn't know anything about a murder and that he was not separated from David on the morning of January 31, 1969, for more than two minutes at any point.

Eight days later, Nichol John was interviewed by detectives in Regina. She confirmed that at no point during the morning of January 31 was she separated from either David or Ron for more than one or two minutes.

But back in Saskatoon, evidence continued to build. On April 4, with most of the snow melted away, Gail

Miller's wallet was found close to the Cadrain house in a neighbour's yard. A bloody toque was also found. The police now had a trail of Gail's belongings leading from the alley, where her body was found, to Shorty Cadrain's house.

What police didn't know, however, was that a few weeks earlier a young neighbour of the Cadrains' had found Larry Fisher's wallet outside in the snow, too. The boy returned the wallet to Larry's wife, Linda. Linda was puzzled; she wondered what Larry's wallet was doing there, and why hadn't he told her he'd lost it?

CHAPTER TEN

TURNING THE TABLES ON DAVID MILGAARD

Ron Wilson was scared. He had a record and didn't want to go back to jail.

The police officer told him someone had come forward and said David Milgaard was the murderer. Ron was fingerprinted, samples of saliva and blood were taken, and he was told to strip and hand over his underwear.

Ron did what he was told. He knew he didn't do anything wrong, but for the police to take that stuff meant they thought he could be the killer. He couldn't just keep his mouth shut and get framed for this crime. He had to give the police what they wanted. It was the only way to get out of this mess.

Nichol John was held overnight in a cell where she freaked out, screaming and crying. A female prison attendant, called a matron, stayed with her to keep her calm. In the morning she and Ron were taken separately to a hotel to take a lie detector test. Ron went through the test first, and then they took a break. During the break the police left Ron and Nichol together in the hallway.

"What did you tell the cops?" Ron asked Nichol.

"The truth, but it's like they don't believe me; they kept me locked up all night."

"Me too. They said Shorty came forward and said David did the murder," said Ron.

"Oh, God! Do you think he did? I mean, we were with him the whole time, how could he?" Nichol looked to Ron for answers.

"Look, he was gone for a while when he screwed up the car. He could have done it then; but whatever. I can't go back to jail, Niki. She was a nurse, sexually assaulted and murdered. You have no idea what inmates do to someone who does that stuff. I just can't go back. I say we just tell them what they want to hear. Let David look after himself."

"So, you think he did it?"

"No, but it doesn't matter what I think. The cops say he did it. I just don't want to get dragged into it with him, ya know?"

"Yeah."

"Let's sink him, just tell the cops what they want to hear," said Ron.

"Yeah," agreed Nichol. David had dumped her and Ron always stuck by her. She had to do this for Ron.

Ron was called back into the room to take the test again. By the end of the second interview, Ron changed his story.

"David told me he did it."

Nichol was next. She was hooked up to a machine with wires, and sat nervously on a chair.

"While on the trip to Saskatoon, were you taking *LSD*?" the detective asked Nichol.

"Yes," she replied. The machine had arms that were moving back and forth and scribbling lines on paper.

"Did David attack anyone on that trip?"

"No, I don't remember that." More scribbling.

The door opened and a police officer walked in. He was carrying a bloody nurse's uniform, which he laid on a table in front of Nichol. She stared at it.

"My God," she said. "I do remember. I do remember. I saw him fighting with her down the lane. I saw him stab her. The car got stuck in an alley, and David and Ron left to go get help. David tried to steal a woman's purse and when she fought him, he dragged her into the alley and stabbed her."

"What did you do when you saw this?" asked Roberts.

She said, "I think I got out of the car and ran."

"Well, where did you run to?"

"I don't know."

"Did you get back in the car? Were you picked up after, or what happened?"

She said, "I must have got back in the car, because I was there when Ron came back, but I don't remember. I was hysterical."

"Where did David get the knife?"

"He broke into a grain elevator, he found it there."

Ron was interrogated next. He said David had stolen a flashlight and a knife from a farm outside Aylesbury, Saskatchewan, on the way to Saskatoon. David probably did the murder. When Ron came back to the car after looking for help, Nichol was hysterical and David had blood on his pants.

The police no longer thought that the murder of Gail Miller was connected to the earlier attacks on women in Saskatoon. David Milgaard wasn't in Saskatoon during the attacks, but he was there when Gail Miller was murdered. To them, this meant that they were still looking for a rapist, but they had their killer.

• • •

A police bulletin went out: David Milgaard was wanted for the murder of Gail Miller.

On May 30, 1969, David was selling subscriptions

in Prince George, British Columbia, when he heard the police wanted him for questioning again. He went to the police station in Prince George. He was interviewed by the same officer who had taken Shorty's revised statement about seeing blood on David's pants. David wasn't going to play with the cops this time. In his gut he knew he was in the worst trouble he'd ever been in before.

"I was scared, and I mean at this point I tried to help the police out on more than one occasion, just offering them the truth," recalled David.

Cooperation didn't help. David Milgaard was charged with non-capital murder for the sexual assault and stabbing of Gail Miller. He was taken back to Saskatoon and put in a holding cell in the city jail. He was fingerprinted and photographed. David refused to sign any forms while in police custody. He talked nonstop, telling them over and over he didn't kill anyone. David was told to strip and hand over his underwear. He did what he was asked and also gave them a saliva sample.

David Milgaard was sixteen at the time of his arrest. He turned seventeen on July 7, 1969, while in prison awaiting trial for the murder of Gail Miller.

Not the happy birthday he had hoped for.

11

CHAPTER ELEVEN

BETRAYED

On January 19, 1970, David Milgaard's family fought their way through the horde of reporters on the steps of the Saskatoon courthouse.

Once inside, David's parents took their seats a couple of rows behind the defence lawyers, along with their son Chris and daughters Maureen and Susan.

David entered the courtroom from a side door and was escorted to the *defendant's* box along the side wall, facing the *jury* along the far wall.

The audience was hushed and everyone stood as the Judge entered the courtroom and took his seat in front.

The Milgaard family were staunch believers in the justice system. They knew a mistake had been made and expected the trial to put an end to this nightmare. They had raised their children to regard the police as their friends. It was inconceivable to them that the police, the judge, or the jury would convict David. Innocent people did not go to prison. David had his problems, but that didn't mean their son was a murderer.

Across from the Milgaards, a few rows behind the *Crown attorney*, sat Gail Miller's parents and some of her nine siblings. They had no reason to believe David wasn't guilty. They were there to see Gail's killer get the punishment he deserved. They wanted closure.

The Crown attorney was Thomas David Roberts Caldwell. David Milgaard's lawyer was Calvin Tallis. Chief Justice Alfred Bence was the judge. A jury would decide David's fate.

Thomas Caldwell examined Nichol John on the witness stand:

"Okay; and you say that you got stuck in an alley behind a funeral home?"

"Yes, into the alley," said Nichol.

"Dave got out and back briefly; what happened then?"

"They both went out."

"They both got out."

"Yes."

"And did you get out?"

"No."

"Alright," said Caldwell. "What happened when the two of them got out?"

"Then they both came back into the car."

Caldwell stopped and looked at Nichol. She wasn't telling the story on her signed statement. She wasn't telling the court about the stabbing and how upset she was. Her signed statement was useless unless she told the same story to the court. He had to push her harder.

"And how much time elapsed between the two of them getting out and the two of them coming back?"

"Only a few minutes," said Nichol.

Caldwell skipped the details that David did not have time to undress Gail, rape her, re-dress her, and then stab her.

Caldwell's frustration with Nichol grew. He jumped to the part where they were at the house and David changed his clothes. She had told the police there was blood on David's pants.

"And Dave changed his pants?" asked Caldwell.

"Right."

"What was done with the pants?"

"Well, Dave's pants I put in his suitcase but I don't know what happened to Ron's."

Caldwell was now angry. He handed Nichol the signed statement she had given the police after the lie detector test and told her to read it. Nichol held it in her shaking hands and read it.

"Now, have you read the entire thing silently through to yourself, Miss John?"

"Yes, I have."

"And I ask you now whether or not you made that statement?"

"I did," said Nichol as tears spilled down her cheeks.

"Are pages three, four, and five true?" Caldwell asked, referring to the blood on David's pants.

"I don't know."

Seeing the frustration building in Caldwell, Judge Bence decided to intervene and try to get to the truth.

"What do you mean you don't know? You signed them," said the judge to Nichol.

"Yeah," Nichol said, sobbing. "I know I did but I don't know. I don't remember saying that."

"You signed the pages, each one at the bottom of the page?" asked the judge.

"Yes."

"And you gave a detailed statement with respect to what you said had taken place, didn't you?"

"Yes."

Nichol looked at David in the defendant's box and the questioning continued until, broken and exhausted, Nichol John was excused.

David watched Nichol leave the stand and was as

confused as she was. Her signed statement said he'd snatched a purse. He hadn't done that. Nichol said he'd stabbed someone. He hadn't done that, either. Why had she lied to the police?

Nichol's denials and the persistent questioning didn't confuse the jury, however. It made them think that Nichol was lying on the stand, and her signed statement was the truth. They said later they believed Nichol John had seen David Milgaard kill Gail Miller.

Ron Wilson took the stand next. He knew what he was going to say, and he was sticking to his story.

"Well, I pulled up and David asked her for directions. She didn't know. I drove straight ahead and tried to make a U-turn, but got stuck."

"And you said you went off to find some help?" prompted Caldwell.

"Yes . . . Dave and me . . . and when I went back to the car she [Nichol] was pretty much hysterical, crying and pretty well screaming. When David got into the car he was breathing fast like he'd been running. He said 'I fixed her.'"

David sat forward in his seat and tried to catch Ron's eye, but Ron wouldn't look at him. Ron was lying. He and Ron were only apart for a couple of minutes when they found those other guys to help push them out.

The only time David was away for longer was when he moved Ron's car and the transmission line broke. He was only away for fifteen minutes, max, and that was after the body was found.

Shorty Cadrain was called as a witness for the Crown. He told the court that when David got to his house on January 31, 1969, his pants were ripped, and there was blood on them. Shorty also said that David's coat was chewed up and he had dumped the bloody clothes in the garbage. Milgaard's defence lawyer, Calvin Tallis, asked Shorty where the blood on David's clothes came from. Shorty refused to give him a straight answer, saying only "it's not nice to say."

David Milgaard sat stunned and sickened that his friends had turned on him. He wanted to testify, but Tallis said he wouldn't make a very good witness and he would do himself more harm than good.

Next the court heard from the police officers who were first on the crime scene. Joyce Milgaard cringed when the court was shown the picture of Gail's body in the snow. She knew David couldn't have done it. But she was a mother, too, and felt deeply the pain she thought Gail's mother must have felt seeing the photo and hearing the graphic details of her daughter's murder.

The police pointed out the position, the fourteen stab

wounds, and the fifteen slashes across Gail's neck. They talked about the weather conditions and the very poor visibility that morning due to the fog. They concluded there were two types of knives used on the victim: one was one-sided and the other two-sided. One was identified as being a paring knife. It had been used so violently, the blade had snapped off in the victim and was later found under the body.

The jury was shown diagrams of the crime scene. They showed the most likely route Gail had taken to her bus stop. They covered the route David and his friends took in their car, and the time it took, including the ten or so minutes David and Ron had left the car. They showed the path of Gail's discarded belongings strewn between the alley and Cadrains' house. The strength of the Crown's case against David lay on this trail and on Nichol's statement that the car was in the alley.

Despite the damning testimony and evidence the police and investigators had introduced to the court, the Milgaards continued to believe David wouldn't be convicted. The twelve jurors who had heard the evidence would see that the witnesses couldn't keep their stories straight. They would know David was innocent. David's mom, Joyce, would later say that while the family was waiting for the jury to reach a *verdict*, even the guards were relaxed. They joked and laughed together. The Milgaards believed they would all go back to their lives soon.

But while they waited they also began to realize that all the evidence hadn't been brought forward. For example, David was left-handed and the stabbing had been done by a right-handed person. Nichol had changed her story three times and none of the versions gave David enough time to commit the assault and murder. Experts had said the assault probably happened in a car, or at least somewhere other than where the body was found. Nichol said she saw David stab a girl once, yet Gail Miller was stabbed fourteen times. Shorty was the only one who had said there was blood on David's pants. If he had committed the murder, then the others would have seen him covered in blood, too.

12

CHAPTER TWELVE

CONVICTED

After eleven days of testimony, the jury reached its decision. On the bailiff's instruction, everyone in the courtroom stood. The judge entered and court was called to order. The jury filed in. David Milgaard, in the defendant's box, tried to look the members of the jury in the eyes, but none even glanced his way.

The judge asked for the verdict. The jury foreman stood. Even the room seemed to hold its breath.

"Guilty," the foreman said.

David looked at his family in disbelief.

"I turned around and I seen my father, who was a very big man. And I seen him look completely weak. And that scared me more than anything else, more than anything I had seen in my life."

The guilty verdict had cut through the Milgaard family like a knife. Joyce dissolved into tears and Lorne put his arm around her as the guards led David out of the courtroom. Gail Miller's father, with tears in his eyes, in a fit of compassion for David's family, reached out and squeezed Lorne's arm before leaving the courtroom.

"I'm sorry," he said.

David Edgar Milgaard was sentenced to life in prison on January 31, 1970, exactly one year after the horrific murder of Gail Miller. He ceased to be a carefree teenager; he was now prisoner number 289699, a convicted rapist and murderer at the age of seventeen. His free spirit was to be locked behind bars without a chance of parole for ten years.

"How could they not see a mistake had been made?" wondered Joyce years later. "David didn't do it. The police had made a mistake and I fully believed they would see the mistake and correct it. We were all so naive back then. In fact, when the police first arrived at my front door in Landenberg, Saskatchewan, looking for David in connection with the Gail Miller rape and murder, I invited them in and gave them coffee. David was innocent; I had nothing to worry about."

Cameras exploded as the Milgaards left the courthouse after the sentencing. Microphones were thrust in their faces. A reporter asked what they would do now, and the question hung in the air for a moment. *What would they do? There were appeals, right? Their lawyers would do what was necessary to get David free, right? There really wasn't anything the family could do to help, was there?*

"Even after the guilty verdict I still had that unwavering faith that this mistake would be seen and corrected through the *appeal* process. It simply did not occur to me that David would not be successful with the appeals," said Joyce years later. "Unfortunately, appeals take months, even years. And lawyers cost money and we didn't have much of that. I suppose it's safe to say the guilty verdict was a shock. The whole family simply was not prepared for it. When David was taken away it was, in some ways, similar to a death. Shock hits, then disbelief, anger, helplessness, hopelessness, and every emotion in between. We were one small family against the justice system of Canada. So small against such a big foe, a foe that was there to protect Canadians from those who would do harm. Months passed and at first it was like living a nightmare. We were used to David travelling, and for a time I still expected him to walk through the door. But he didn't."

On February 21, 1970, while David was waiting to be transferred to the federal penitentiary in Prince Albert, Saskatchewan, another woman in the Pleasant Hill neighbourhood was sexually assaulted at knifepoint.

13

CHAPTER THIRTEEN

REALITY

David Milgaard was innocent and every night he went to sleep hoping to wake from his horrible dream. Every morning he awoke to another day still trapped in his nightmare.

On March 2, 1970, David received the first of many reality checks. He was moved from the provincial jail and transferred to a federal penitentiary. Provincial jails house people whose sentences are less than two years. Penitentiaries are for longer sentences and usually for worse crimes. David's new home was a one-by-two-and-a-half-metre cell in the federal penitentiary in Prince Albert, Saskatchewan. His nightmare was now his life, and it was turning from bad to worse.

His first sight of his new "home" was forbidding. The massive rock fortress, complete with gun towers and armed patrols, made his blood run cold. He was handcuffed and shackled. He got out of the transport on command and was escorted through a chain-link fence with rolls of barbed wire at the top. He was ushered inside. Every door was locked, every entrance surveyed, and dozens of eyes watched him. David was very frightened. He was stripped, searched, and then assigned prison clothing and a cell. The clang of the cell door as it shut behind him for the first time was a sound that echoed in David's head for the next twenty-three years of hell.

David's cell contained a toilet, a sink, two or three attached metal book shelves, and a hinged bed that could be folded up against the wall. His cell was at the end of a long hall near the telephone where he listened to inmates yelling and cursing at their families. They wanted visits, they wanted money, and they wanted drugs. Or worse, he listened to them crying into the telephone receiver.

At first he told himself the officials would let him out because he was innocent and they would see that. Then, when time passed and he was still there, he told himself his lawyers would get him out with the appeal.

On January 5, 1971, David's first appeal of his conviction was dismissed by the Saskatchewan Court of Appeal. David, already plagued by depression, frustration, and disappointment, tried to commit suicide. The prison arranged for a counsellor to help him through

the disappointments. It didn't help. The counsellor tried
to help David admit to the murder so he could move
on and deal with prison life. David was innocent and
wouldn't admit guilt.

The prison system moved him from Prince Albert
Penitentiary to Stony Mountain Prison in Manitoba. It
was harder for family to visit him there and his depression
grew. He tried to commit suicide again and was sexually
assaulted by other inmates. David learned to defy the
guards now and again so he could be thrown into solitary
confinement. It was the only place he was safe, the only
place he found peace. It was like a holiday from prison.

On August 31, 1977, David was formally denied day
parole, because he still didn't admit his guilt.

The justice system had found him guilty. So when
David declared his innocence, or reacted badly to appeals
being denied, he sank further and further into depression. Prison psychiatrists misdiagnosed him with mental
illnesses because they believed he was running from his
guilt. He was sent to mental institutions after suicide
attempts and given medications that clouded his thinking.

It felt like no one was listening to him. No one except
for his family, especially his mother, Joyce.

Joyce and Lorne Milgaard still believed in the appeal
process. Joyce wrote letters and met with lawyers as much

as she could. She was still raising a family, and the legal bills had to be paid. The family didn't know what more they could do.

On June 19, 1979, David was permitted to apply for full parole. His lawyers and the prison counsellor explained that he'd have to admit to his crime and show remorse. David was furious. He told them all yet again that he couldn't admit to murdering someone when he hadn't done it. He was innocent. How could he show remorse for doing such an unspeakable horror to someone when he hadn't done it?

His parole was denied.

14

CHAPTER FOURTEEN

ON THE RUN

Compared to other inmates, David was a co-operative prisoner. After twelve years in prison, the authorities felt it was time to grant him a chaperoned day pass on August 22, 1980, for his brother Chris's twenty-seventh birthday. David was ecstatic. For the first time in twelve years he would be able to feel the wind on his face without seeing the prison walls.

David's prison guard was made to feel at home when he brought David to the apartment complex where his parents lived. David was polite and respectful and made sure the guard knew where he was at all times. The man relaxed.

The family was out on the apartment deck for a barbecue when David and his sister, Maureen, accompanied by the guard, went down to the public games room for a game of pool. They were almost finished their second game when Maureen asked the guard if she could have a few private minutes with her brother. Since the game was almost over, he agreed.

"Tell Dad we'll be there in just a minute," said David as he bent over the table for another shot. The guard said later, "I trusted him."

Maureen went to the window of the games room and watched the guard disappear from sight.

"Maureen," David told his sister. "I can't go back. Drive me to town so I can disappear. And when you get back, tell everyone I forced you so they can't charge you with anything." Maureen didn't hesitate. She wanted David to be free. She knew that David was innocent and that being in prison was a living hell for him. They ran to Maureen's car and were gone in minutes.

The guard was in the Milgaard apartment for about ten minutes before he started getting concerned. Finally, he went back to the games room and found it empty. He checked the parking lot and Maureen's car was gone. With a sinking feeling, he called the prison. In minutes, an all-points bulletin was out for David Milgaard and for Maureen's car.

"There really wasn't any other motivator other than the fact that I felt I was dying inside prison. Every day, I was dying a little bit more," said David years later. "After a while, when people keep telling you 'you did this' after years you start thinking, did I? And then you start losing yourself and going a bit crazy."

David Milgaard was now an escaped fugitive.

Before the guard had a chance to call in the escape, the two had already stopped at a pharmacy where Maureen bought blond hair dye. Then, while Maureen purchased David a ticket at the bus station, David went into the restroom with the dye. Dark-haired, dark-eyed David Milgaard had walked into the restroom, but a twenty-eight-year-old blond man named Dave McAdam walked out and boarded a bus to Toronto.

Once the bus was out of sight, Maureen used a pay phone to call home. She pretended to cry and said David had forced her to help him escape to the west coast. Then she drove home to the myriad of questions awaiting her.

The police focused their search to the west. Television and radio stations all broke the news that convicted murderer David Milgaard had escaped. Photos of Gail Miller's murdered body flashed across television screens. Calls of sightings lit up the phones of police stations across Canada, but mostly in the west. Meanwhile, David had made his way east. Toronto was a huge city; he thought it was the perfect place to hide.

• • •

While David Milgaard was on the run, something surprising happened. On August 28, 1980, Linda Fisher, then Larry's ex-wife, decided the time had come to tell the police she suspected Larry had killed Gail Miller. Linda confessed the events that occurred at her home on the morning of Gail Miller's murder. She told officers that she and Larry had argued that day when he got home. Even then, with the news of the murder on the radio, she had angrily accused her husband of having stolen her kitchen knife and killing the woman. She told them about Larry's wallet, which the neighbour boy had returned. She said she believed David Milgaard was innocent.

Why had Linda Fisher come forward?

In September 1970, her husband had finally been caught and sent to prison for rape. The family had left Saskatoon and was living in Fort Garry, Winnipeg. While in police custody, Larry admitted to another rape and an attempted rape in Saskatoon. A Saskatchewan police officer was notified of Larry's admission and travelled to Winnipeg to interview him. But because David Milgaard had already been convicted of Gail's murder, police did not connect the dots that pointed to Larry as the real killer. Larry was released on January 26, 1980, and on March 31, he assaulted a woman in North Battleford, Saskatchewan, and was again arrested.

A police officer took Linda Fisher's statement, but filed it away.

• • •

Once in Toronto, David Milgaard rented a room in a boarding house and found a job selling encyclopaedias over the telephone. It only lasted a little over a month. He started dating a sixteen-year-old girl named Rhonda. She was still in high school and her parents didn't know about David. She knew he was twenty-eight and had been in trouble with the law. She didn't know he was an escaped prisoner.

Rhonda would take the bus into the city after school to spend time with David. On the weekends, they spent their days panhandling for food since he was always short of cash. David did short-term work in a string of nowhere jobs — pumping gas, running errands, doing yard work — to earn enough to pay for his rent. He couldn't give his social insurance number out for work, so he was limited in what he could do without getting caught. But he was happy. The frustration melted away, and so did his depression. Without the medication from prison doctors, he could think clearly and he relaxed.

David called his mother a number of times to let her know he was okay. Joyce never told the police. She managed to sneak away from home and, wearing a wig, she flew to Toronto to see him and take him shopping for clothes. They both knew it couldn't last, but neither of them knew how to fix the situation. They both hoped that the truth would come out so he wouldn't have to stay in hiding for the rest of his life.

Another phone call changed the course of David's life again. This one was anonymous. "Hi," said the anonymous caller to the Toronto police. "I just want to let you know that David Milgaard is living here in Toronto. He's got a sawed-off shotgun, and he's planning on robbing a bank. He said if anyone tried to stop him, he'd blow their head off."

David was unarmed and had no such plans. The police, however, took the caller at his word.

It wasn't too hard for the police to find David. In a joint investigation with the RCMP, the Toronto police located him. On November 8, 1980, as David was walking down Queen Street in the west end of the city, Corporal Jack Briscoe of the RCMP yelled out for him to stop. Startled, David ducked into an alley. The police had him cornered. They had all been told David was armed and dangerous, which wasn't the case. David wasn't carrying any weapons. Briscoe came around the corner of the alley and yelled for him to stop as he levelled his revolver at David's back. David stopped and fell to his knees. There was a crack from the firearm, and David felt the sting in his back. The police had shot an unarmed man.

David was handcuffed and taken by ambulance to St. Joseph's Hospital.

As he lay in a hospital room with a bullet lodged against his spine, he was told he might never walk again. As soon as he could be moved, he would be returning to prison. His freedom had lasted seventy-seven days.

15

CHAPTER FIFTEEN

THE FIGHT

Sitting next to her son in his hospital room, Joyce came to the realization that there would be no miracle *acquittal* for David. She decided she needed to fight harder than she had ever fought in her life, if David was to be freed.

When David left the hospital on crutches, he was sent to the Kingston Penitentiary in Ontario. He was defiant and refused medical treatment. Drugs had helped ruin his life and he felt he needed to use his determination, not painkillers, to heal his body. While he passed up the painkillers, he made a pail of an alcoholic concoction — from fermented bread and either potato peelings or fruit — called jailhouse hooch. He drank that to help with the pain. It was found, and he landed in solitary confinement for ten days — crutches and all. David used the time to exercise and build up the strength in his legs. He was determined to prove the doctors wrong. If and when he finally left prison, he wanted it to be on his own two legs.

On December 28, 1988, David made his first application to the federal justice minister to review his conviction. It was dismissed on February 27, 1991, and a month later, David's application for parole was turned down. Another blow.

From Kingston, David was transferred to Millhaven, a maximum-security prison in Bath, Ontario. David started looking to the future. His stint on the run reminded him of how important freedom was. He wanted that freedom back, and he knew he needed to put his life on a positive track. He decided to stay out of trouble and put time and energy into his education. He enrolled in some courses through the prison, and started feeling good about himself. David also started a support group in the prison, and brought in speakers to talk about how prisoners can help themselves through the legal process.

That was only part of David's focus. He still wanted out of jail. There wasn't much he could do from behind bars. It wasn't as if he could knock on doors or hunt down the real killer. However, he could write letters. To that end, he wrote to the two people who knew the truth and who could get people to listen.

May 1, 1981

Nichol

*From our energetic shuffling inside a sleeping bag in
Victoria Park to the inadequate coupling in a hotel
of so long ago, all of this before the 12 years of living
inside 4 walls in a room like your bathroom, Niki, do
you have any idea of who I am today?*

*I'm only going to tell you once, I am a 25 year old
man that still believes in human good and I'm also
very tired. I don't know how it's been for you all this
time to know that I never killed anyone, but for me it
has been murder.*

*Regardless of whoever, or however things were arranged
or rearranged so long ago, the truth will always remain
the same. When I saw you on the stand I said to
myself they must have really screwed you around. My
mom and dad had hardly anything then and today
what they do have they are putting behind me because
they know I cannot handle anymore prison. Niki, don't
make them waste everything,*

Please help them just by telling

Them

The

Truth.

Sincerely,

David Milgaard

CHAPTER SIXTEEN

JOYCE TAKES CHARGE

Together, David and Joyce Milgaard spent hours carefully going over details of David's trip to Saskatoon in 1969. She made lists of witnesses and then tracked them down. Lawyers were expensive, as were ads in papers and private investigators. Travelling took another chunk of their finances and most of the time doors were slammed in her face and telephone conversations were abruptly ended. The family was running out of money.

The battle took its toll on David's parents' marriage. They split, but they still fought for David together. Joyce was away so much; Lorne was the one who had to be there for the other kids. But he supported the fight.

Eventually, it paid off and the tide started to change.

Joyce met with the prime minister at the time, Brian Mulroney, NDP leader Audrey McLaughlin, media, and politicians. She contacted anyone she felt might be able to help. She even wrote a letter to Queen Elizabeth. Magazines and newspapers picked up the story of her fight. Joyce worked hard to keep the media involved. Mothers across Canada were beginning to see her desperation to save her child, and sympathized with her.

Witnesses were tracked down, and posters and flyers were made up offering rewards for information. Tips started pouring in. Through a private investigator hired by the Milgaards, Joyce found out about Larry Fisher having lived in the basement suite of the Cadrain house. She found out he was behind bars for assaulting women. All the pieces fit. Joyce had found the key to freeing David. They now knew Gail Miller's killer. They just had to prove it.

The first step was to prove David was innocent and to do that, they needed new evidence.

The Milgaards' lawyer, David Asper, appealed for mercy to Kim Campbell, Minister of Justice, on the grounds of new evidence not heard or available during the first trial. The new evidence was a brand new DNA test. Time dragged while they awaited the minister's response to new evidence and material found. Copies were sent to Kim Campbell, who told them that all this paperwork only slowed the process and refused anymore submissions. Joyce was furious. She had a forensic report which excluded David from Gail Miller's crime scene and she was determined that the minister of justice was going to see it.

A big break came when Kim Campbell came to Winnipeg. Armed with the report, Joyce called the media to let them know of her plans to confront the minister. They came out in droves.

Positioning themselves at a prime location in the hotel where Kim Campbell was due to arrive, Joyce and David's sister, Maureen, waited with the report in hand. Also waiting were reporters with cameras and microphones, and film crews ready to record the drama they knew was coming.

The tension mounted as the whisper spread that the minister would step into the hallway in seconds. A hush fell on the group as the light above the elevator made its way one floor at a time. Campbell had the fate of David in her hands. Joyce knew she had hundreds, maybe even thousands, of supporters. But they weren't enough. This might well be David's last chance.

The elevator doors opened, microphones were shoved into Kim Campbell's face, and flash bulbs went off. Joyce had no chance to utter a word. Ms. Campbell's hand went up as she recognized Joyce and realized she was being ambushed. All of Canada then heard the words of the minister, as she breezed past Joyce and Maureen Milgaard and verbally pushed Joyce aside.

"Madam," said Kim Campbell, "if you wish to have your son's case dealt with fairly, please do not approach me." She disappeared down the hall.

Joyce almost dropped to the ground as disappointment washed over her. Her chance to free David was gone.

CHAPTER SEVENTEEN

THE BEGINNING OF THE END

Dear Albert,

I hear that the investigator met with you a while ago to have a talk with you. It sounds like we all became victims of what happened and that we are all still "hurting" today.

I want you to know that the past 21 years have been real hell for me. I didn't kill that nurse and hopefully the truth will come out. Everyone keeps asking me if I'm mad at the people who testified against me and I can tell you that nothing is farther from the truth. I'm not mad at you or anyone else. With all the stuff going on with the police I imagine a lot of people said a lot of things.

All I want is to get out of this jail and get on with my life. Maybe we could be friends again man, but I hear you're in B.C. and of course I'm out here. If you can do anything to help that would be all right and if not that's okay too, man.

Peace

David Milgaard

• • •

"I didn't know it then. But when Kim Campbell verbally shoved me aside, it was the turning point for David," Joyce Milgaard recalled later. "Up to then I had the support and sympathy of Canadian mothers who understood the need to fight and protect our children. But now I also had the support of truck drivers and other men across the nation who saw me in the light of their own mothers. They called in to talk shows, wrote letters to the editors of newspapers, started and signed petitions, and wrote letters to Kim Campbell. The people spoke and even though she was the justice minister, she was still a politician and the negative publicity endangered her career. Her actions put David's case on the fast track."

David's lawyer was cautious. He told Joyce not to

approach Kim Campbell again. He didn't want to alien-
ate her with the bad publicity. He was worried it could
backfire and hurt David's case.

Talk shows followed, as well as more newspaper
articles and interviews, and finally a concert was put
together by some musicians from a local folk festival who
wanted to do something for the Milgaards. Joyce had
already written a song for David and while she was told
she couldn't talk to Kim Campbell, she figured she could
at least sing to her. And sing she did, with words like:
"Please Madame Minister, set David free," and "Twenty-
one years of torment and pain. Twenty-one years can't
be brought back again," and ending finally with, "Please
Madame Minister, set my son free."

CBC's *the fifth estate* broadcast "Who Killed Gail
Miller?" on September 25, 1990. In that documentary
Ron Wilson stated he had lied about seeing blood on
David's clothes and lied about the knife. "I was scared
that if they weren't going to charge David with this, they
were going to charge me."

Larry Fisher's ex-wife, Linda, was also interviewed.
She spoke about going to the police in 1980 and telling
them about the fight she'd had with Larry the morning
of the killing and about the missing paring knife. The
show also aired the news clip of Kim Campbell brushing

past Joyce Milgaard, and aired the song Joyce had written to the minister. Perhaps it aired too much. The appeal to the justice department was turned down on February 21, 1991.

Years before, the Milgaards had hired an organization called Centurion Ministries. It was their goal to help free the wrongfully convicted. Their investigators and Joyce had conducted and taped interviews of witnesses in regards to the murder of Gail Miller. Subsequently, the Miller family had been sent these tapes. Gail Miller's family, after watching them, submitted a public written statement supporting the need for a fresh look at the twenty-one-year-old murder case.

On September 6, 1991, a vigil was organized in front of the hotel where Prime Minister Brian Mulroney was scheduled to speak. Joyce Milgaard approached the prime minister's staff to assure them the vigil would be peaceful and none of them would harass or approach the prime minister.

The prime minister, it seemed, had other ideas.

Prime Minister Mulroney walked over to Joyce to have a few words with her.

Years later, in an interview with the *Winnipeg Free Press*, Mulroney was quoted as saying:

There was just something so forlorn but very
loving about a woman standing alone on a
very cold evening in Manitoba on behalf of her
son. But in that brief meeting I got a sense of
Mrs. Milgaard and her genuineness and her
courage. We all have mothers. But even the
most devoted and loving of mothers would not
continue their crusade for twenty-two years if
there was any doubt in her mind. So I went
back to Ottawa and had a much closer look at
it . . . I told the appropriate people I thought
a review of this particular case was warranted
and I wanted appropriate action taken to bring
this about.

— *Interviewed by Gordon Sinclair Jr.,*
Winnipeg Free Press, *July 29, 1997*

Not long after her quiet conversation with the prime
minister, Joyce received a phone call from David.

"Hello," Joyce said.

"They moved me out of the Pen," said David.
Mulroney had looked into David's case and that little
conversation resulted in David's move out of the penitentiary. "I'm at Rockwood Farm. It's minimum security
here. They let me go outside, Mom. Mom, I stood outside

and for the first time in so many years, I watched the sun set, saw the whole thing with the breeze blowing on my skin and no bars between me and the rest of the world, oh, Mom!" David was crying and so was his mother.

David Milgaard's case was reopened and referred to the Supreme Court of Canada on November 29, 1991.

Rather than incur the expense of reopening such an old case, the Saskatchewan government decided to simply release David Milgaard. After all, he had served twenty-three years for murder, so he'd done his time, whether he admitted the crime or not. He wasn't found innocent, so no apology was necessary. He wasn't paroled, so there was no need for a parole officer to help him get a job, housing, and re-established in society. Neat, simple, done.

Or was it?

18

CHAPTER EIGHTEEN

FREEDOM

David Milgaard, aged thirty-nine, left the prison for the last time shortly after 12 p.m. on April 16, 1992. He had been a prisoner longer than he had been a free man. All he owned was the money he had banked while in prison, a little more than $200. Things on the outside had changed drastically in twenty-three years. He didn't have a driver's licence, a bank account, a credit card, or even a credit rating. He'd never rented a house or owned his own car. He hadn't danced at his high school graduation or been taken out by friends when he became old enough to legally drink. Technology had moved on without him, and social rules had changed. When asked what he did for a living, what could he say?

David was out of prison, but since he was never cleared of the crime, he was still a convicted murderer. The Milgaards knew the fight wouldn't be over until they proved David was innocent.

It took some time, but on July 18, 1997, a British laboratory confirmed that the semen samples extracted from pieces of Gail Miller's clothing did not originate from David Milgaard, and were very likely to have originated from Larry Fisher.

This scientific evidence proved to the world what the Milgaards had always known: David Milgaard did not kill Gail Miller. Thirty years after the murder, a settlement of ten million dollars was issued to David Milgaard in compensation for being wrongly convicted. The Saskatchewan government said: "We're sorry."

On November 22, 1999, justice was served. Larry Fisher was convicted of the sexual assault and murder of Gail Miller and sentenced to life without parole until 2010.

All of David's supporters asked how an innocent man could spend all that time in prison for a crime he didn't commit. The general public asked how and why this had happened. The questions and facts about this case were splashed across newspapers, on television, and considered through all avenues of the media. The pressure was on. If this could happen to David, who else could this happen, or had this happened, to?

Finally, the Saskatchewan government gave in. On Friday, February 20, 2004, Minister of Justice Frank

Quennel announced that the Honourable Mr. Justice Edward P. MacCallum of the Alberta Court of Queen's Bench would conduct an inquiry into any and all aspects of the investigation into the death of Gail Miller. The inquiry would also include examining the criminal proceedings resulting in the wrongful conviction of David Edgar Milgaard. The Commission of Inquiry would decide whether the investigation should have been reopened based on information subsequently received by the police and the department of justice.

The Commission of Inquiry began in 2005 and lasted for 191 days. During the Inquiry, 114 witnesses were interviewed and nineteen others were "read in." (Some witnesses were not available or were deceased at the time of the Inquiry, as in the case of Albert Cadrain, who passed away in 1995. In these instances their previously written statements would be used.) In addition, there were 3,200 documents, including police reports and trial testimony. On completion, the Inquiry filled 193 volumes for a total of 40,541 pages. There were a number of recommendations to improve the Canadian justice system, but there was no blame laid on any law enforcement officials.

The statement David Milgaard made to the Inquiry on April 24, 2006, included:

I want everyone to know there are many victims from this tragedy. I hope the court is able to see this, and to try to offer what care it can for these people where they can. Ronald Wilson and Nichol John are just a few of the many that need this kindness . . .

All I can say is thank you very much to all the legal people that have been helping me out, my legal teams: there are quite a few of them over the years.

I think it's important to say one thing that comes to mind. You know, a lot of Canadian people have come up to my family, myself, my mother, and they come up to us and they congratulate us, still, and they ask me how I am, how my mum is. I think it's important for them to know . . . David Milgaard, Joyce Milgaard, they're not so important as what you see in these people's faces . . . you see the love come up in their faces, and what that is, really, is just them caring for what's right and what's just. So even though I apologize for this case taking as long as it has for this country, maybe it's done a lot of people some good somehow, because they care about what's right and just, and I think that's important to Canada. Thank you.

EPILOGUE: WHERE ARE THEY NOW?

DAVID MILGAARD is married with two children and lives in Calgary, Alberta. He is in his sixties and is the primary caregiver to his children. In a Facebook message to the author, David said he only wants a normal life and to put all this behind him. However, that is not easy to do, as the media continues to document his every move.

After he received the compensation package (which he shared with his family), he took flying lessons with his mother and bought her an airplane. David presented his friend and lawyer, David Asper, with a brand new Harley Davidson motorcycle as a thank you for helping him in his fight with the Canadian justice system. David is happy and settled, as much as one can be after having twenty-three years of his youth stolen. He says that he has put all of this behind him.

JOYCE MILGAARD is very active in the Church of
Christian Science. She gives her faith the credit for getting her through this mammoth ordeal. In her home
office is a crystal plaque: an honorary Doctorate of Law
from the University of Manitoba. She has become a
role model for many Canadians. She was added to the
Maclean's Magazine's Honour Roll. She was also awarded
the Commemorative Medal for the 125th Anniversary
of Confederation in 1992 for "significant contribution
to fellow citizens, their community, or Canada." Joyce
has been very active with the John Howard Society and
continues to sit on the board of directors of AIDWYC.
She and David Asper founded the Manitoba chapter. In
1999, Joyce wrote the book *A Mother's Story: The Fight
to Free My Son David*, with the help of author Peter
Edwards. This book quickly became a best-seller.

LORNE MILGAARD, David's father, worked hard in
the background and took his family responsibili-
ties very seriously. He was the reason why Joyce was
able to do so much. Lorne was a big, quiet, physically
strong man. After David received his compensation,
Joyce and Lorne moved into a house in Petersfield,
Manitoba. They were still separated, but enjoyed a few
quieter years than the past three decades. On Monday,
December 10, 2007, Lorne passed away at the age of

seventy-eight, after years of heart problems.

LARRY FISHER was found guilty of Gail Miller's murder on November 22, 1999, and was sentenced on January 4, 2000. He is still in prison. He has spent a total of twenty-five years in jail for various rapes he committed in Manitoba and Saskatchewan.

ALBERT (SHORTY) CADRAIN was diagnosed with a mental illness four years after David Milgaard was convicted. He was institutionalized for a short time after proclaiming he was the son of God. He struggled with his mental illness for years. In 1995, he was killed in a hunting accident.

RONALD WILSON was cited for contempt by the Supreme Court of Canada in 1992. He dropped out of sight after that.

NICHOL JOHN married, changed her name, and moved away. She has buried her past and the author was unable to find any updated information about her.

GAIL MILLER should never be forgotten.

ACKNOWLEDGEMENTS

I would like to thank AIDWYC and their representative, Win Wahrer, Director of Client Services, who was kind enough to write the foreword for this book and put up with all my questions. Also Centurion Ministries in the United States, who gave me vital information for tracking down information and encouragement in the writing of this book. Saskatchewan Penitentiary provided the specifics for the cells: thank you so much. Of course, this list would not be complete without mentioning Joyce Milgaard and her children. Her patience and encouragement in the writing of this book have been invaluable, and the suggestions from her children were unexpected and very much appreciated. Thank you so much, Mrs. Milgaard. I wish you, David, and all your family a rich and wonderful future.

TIMELINE

OCTOBER 21, 1968: Victim One is raped by Larry Fisher.

NOVEMBER 13, 1968: Victim Two is raped by Fisher.

NOVEMBER 29, 1968: Victim Three is indecently assaulted.

JANUARY 31, 1969: Gail Miller is raped and murdered. David Milgaard, Ron Wilson, and Nichol John are travelling through Saskatoon.

MAY 30, 1969: David Milgaard, age sixteen, turns himself in to police in Prince George, BC.

JANUARY 31, 1970: The Saskatchewan court convicts David Milgaard in the killing of nursing assistant Gail Miller. He is sentenced to life in prison, on the anniversary of Gail Miller's murder.

JULY 1970: Fisher goes to work in Fort Garry, Manitoba.

SEPTEMBER 19, 1970: Fisher is arrested while raping Victim Six in Fort Garry. He confesses and later pleads guilty to the two Manitoba attacks. He also mentions attacking women in Saskatoon.

JANUARY 31, 1971: Saskatchewan Court of Appeal rejects Milgaard's appeal.

NOVEMBER 15, 1971: Supreme Court of Canada refuses to hear Milgaard's appeal.

DECEMBER 21, 1971: Fisher is transferred back to Saskatchewan, where he pleads guilty to all the attacks in a Regina court.

AUGUST 28, 1980: Fisher's ex-wife, Linda, goes to the police with her suspicions about Fisher possibly killing Miller. The investigation is not reopened.

AUGUST 1980: David Milgaard doesn't return to prison after being released on a day pass. He is found in Toronto seventy-seven days later and shot in the back while running from the RCMP.

SEPTEMBER 17, 1984: Brian Mulroney is elected prime minister, a position he will hold until June 24, 1993.

DECEMBER 28, 1988: Milgaard's lawyers apply to have the case reopened.

MAY 14, 1990: Federal Justice Minister Kim Campbell brushes past Milgaard's mother, Joyce.

FEBRUARY 27, 1991: Campbell turns down Milgaard's request to review his case.

AUGUST 14, 1991: Milgaard's lawyers file second application to minister of justice to have the case reopened.

NOVEMBER 29, 1991: Minister of justice refers the Milgaard case for review by the Supreme Court of Canada.

JANUARY 16, 1992: Milgaard's conviction is reviewed by the Supreme Court. Milgaard is freed on the grounds there is enough reasonable doubt to question his conviction.

JANUARY 21, 1992: Milgaard testifies to his innocence as the Supreme Court begins its review.

APRIL 16, 1992: The Supreme Court of Canada says Milgaard should have a new trial. He is released, and the Saskatchewan government decides not to prosecute him again. He is not formally acquitted.

MAY 29, 1993: David Milgaard files a statement of claim in Court of Queen's Bench for malicious prosecution.

JULY 18, 1997: A new round of DNA testing, done in Britain, clears Milgaard and points to Larry Fisher. The Saskatchewan government apologizes to David Milgaard for the wrongful conviction.

JULY 25, 1997: Larry Fisher is arrested in Calgary for the rape and murder of Gail Miller.

MAY 17, 1999: Milgaard and his family receive a $10,000,000 compensation package from the federal government, seven years after he was released from prison.

OCTOBER 12, 1999: The trial for Larry Fisher begins in Yorkton, Saskatchewan.

NOVEMBER 22, 1999: Fisher is convicted of Miller's
murder on the strength of the DNA evidence. He is
sentenced to life in prison.

JANUARY 17, 2005: The public inquiry into
the wrongful conviction of David Milgaard opens
in Saskatoon. Alberta Justice Edward MacCallum is
presiding.

SEPTEMBER 26, 2008: MacCallum releases an
800-page inquiry report. Mistakes are found, but finds
no grounds to suggest any professional misconduct was
carried out by police or *prosecutors*. He states that flawed
media pressure and inaccurate reporting may have alien-
ated people who should have reopened Milgaard's case.

GLOSSARY

ACQUITTAL: the verdict when someone accused of a crime is found not guilty.

APPEAL: a request to review a case that has already been decided in court.

CONVICTION: the verdict when someone accused of a crime is found guilty.

CROWN ATTORNEY: the lawyer acting for the government, or "the Crown," in court proceedings. They are the prosecutors in Canada's legal system.

DEFENDANT: the person who has been formally accused of and charged with committing a crime.

DNA (Deoxyribonucleic acid): a microscopic, double-stranded element in the cells of the body. It is unique to each individual, except for identical twins. DNA determines everything from the colour of your eyes to which diseases you might develop in your life. In the legal system it's been hailed as the greatest advance in investigations since the fingerprint. A fleck of skin, a strand of hair, blood, or other body fluids found at a crime scene can provide a sample of DNA. The sample can be compared to one taken from an accused person, to see if they match. A DNA profile takes up to three months of lab work to produce.

JURY: A criminal trial is decided by a group of twelve

randomly selected citizens from the province in which the trial is held. All twelve must agree on a verdict.

LSD (Lysergic Acid Diethylamide): a powerful drug that causes hallucinations.

PROSECUTOR: the lawyer acting for the prosecution, usually the state (in Canada, the Crown). The prosecutor tries to prove the defendant is guilty.

TESTIMONY: the statement of a witness under oath.

VERDICT: the decision of the jury at the end of a trial, usually guilty or not guilty.

FURTHER READING

ONLINE

For the reader who wishes to find out more about this fascinating case, a rich resource of documents, news articles, and videos is available online through the following links:

www.milgaardinquiry.ca

www.cbc.ca/archives

www.aidwyc.org

INTERMEDIATE LEVEL

Collier, David. *Surviving Saskatoon*. Montreal: Drawn and Quarterly, 2000.

Milgaard, Joyce and Peter Edwards. *A Mother's Story: The Fight To Free My Son David*. Toronto: Doubleday Canada, 1999, and Seal Books, 2000.

NEWSPAPER ARTICLES

Calgary20.ca article by Samantha Thiessen (2009).

The Globe and Mail article by Kirk Makin (1995).

Winnipeg Free Press article by David Asper (1991).

FILM/VIDEO

Milgaard. TV docudrama. Directed by Stephen Williams. 1999. [Best Movie of the Year, 1999 Gemini Awards]

The David Milgaard Story. Directed by Vic Sarin. 1992.
"Who Killed Gail Miller." CBC's *the fifth estate.* 1990.

MUSIC

Canadian musical group The Tragically Hip wrote and
recorded a song named "Wheat Kings" with references to David on their 1992 album *Fully Completely.*

At the Winnipeg Music Festival in 2000, the Winnipeg
Symphony Orchestra played a newly written symphony titled "Milgaard."

PHOTO CREDITS

We gratefully acknowledge the following sources for permission to reproduce the images contained within this book:

CP Images: p. 48 (bottom)

Joyce Milgaard: p. 45, 46 (top and bottom)

Ken Faught/ *Toronto Star* (Nov. 29, 1991): p. 49

Saskatoon *StarPhoenix*: cover, p. 47 (top and bottom), 48 (top)

INDEX